anythink

SPACE DISCOVERY GUIDES

MARS MISSIONS

A SPACE DISCOVERY GUIDE

Buffy Silverman

Lerner Publications ◆ Minneapolis

Lerner Publications Company
A division of Lerner Publishing Group, Inc.
241 First Avenue North
Minneapolis, MN 55401 USA

For reading levels and more information, look up this title at www.lernerbooks.com.

Main body text set in Avenir LT Std 65 Medium 11.5/17.5.
Typeface provided by Adobe Systems.

Library of Congress Cataloging-in-Publication Data

Names: Silverman, Buffy, author.
Title: Mars missions : a space discovery guide / Buffy Silverman.
Description: Minneapolis : Lerner Publications, [2017] | Series: Space discovery
    guides | Audience: Ages 9–12. | Audience: Grades 4 to 6. | Includes
    bibliographical references and index.
Identifiers: LCCN 2016018635 (print) | LCCN 2016023000 (ebook) | ISBN
    9781512425857 (lb : alk. paper) | ISBN 9781512427950 (eb pdf)
Subjects: LCSH: Space flight to Mars—Juvenile literature. | Roving vehicles
    (Astronautics)—Juvenile literature. | Mars (Planet)—Exploration—Juvenile
    literature.
Classification: LCC TL799.M3 S55 2017 (print) | LCC TL799.M3 (ebook) | DDC
    523.43—dc23

LC record available at https://lccn.loc.gov/2016018635

Manufactured in the United States of America
1-41353-23297-6/27/2016

TABLE OF CONTENTS

DREAMING OF MARS

As the nearest Earthlike planet, Mars has long captured our imaginations. Humans have always looked for ways to explore the Red Planet.

In 2001 a businessman in the United States, Elon Musk, began thinking about what kind of business he should become involved in next. He had already been successful with the Internet company PayPal, but he wanted to try something new. Musk, who had always been fascinated by space, began to wonder why people hadn't already traveled to Mars. He stayed up late one night, researching when the United States was planning to send astronauts on a mission to Mars. He found that the National Aeronautics and Space Administration (NASA) had no real plans for a manned mission to Mars. So Musk decided to make the plans himself. He came up with ideas for first sending mice and a greenhouse to Mars. He researched rockets. And when he found out how expensive it would be to buy a rocket, he decided to make his own. The next year he started SpaceX, a company whose goal is to set up human colonies on other planets.

SpaceX has already created and launched its own rockets and spacecraft. The company also works with NASA to bring supplies to the International Space Station (ISS). In 2016 Musk announced that SpaceX plans to send a spacecraft called the *Red Dragon* to Mars in 2018—and the company plans to send people there in 2024.

Musk believes that sending people to Mars is important for the future of humanity and Earth.

Musk poses with a SpaceX craft designed to carry astronauts in space.

A future Mars colony may look similar to the one depicted in this illustration.

He thinks a mission to Mars would be inspiring. By working to reach Mars, people will develop new technologies and make scientific discoveries. Building a colony on Mars "would be a great adventure," Musk said.

Musk also believes that problems on Earth are a big part of the reason why people need to go to Mars. "I think there is a strong humanitarian argument for making life multi-planetary, in order to safeguard the existence of humanity in the event that something catastrophic were to happen," he said. Musk believes that people need to be able to live on other planets to survive if a major disaster occurs on Earth.

Meanwhile, NASA has also announced a plan to send astronauts on a mission to Mars. In 2015 NASA said it would send humans to Mars by the 2030s. Their plan is known as Journey to Mars, and it involves several steps of research and testing on the ISS and in deep space (the area of space beyond Earth and the moon) before people go to Mars. Unlike SpaceX, NASA does not plan to send people to Mars to live long term. Instead, NASA would make multiple visits to the Red Planet with several different crews of astronauts.

Many people are skeptical about whether the missions will actually work. They think sending people to Mars seems too expensive and dangerous. On Earth, people need water and oxygen to survive. On Mars the air and soil are different from Earth's. From a distance, Mars looks as if it is filled with red dirt, not blue water. Could these conditions ever support life?

This is a question people have been asking about Mars for years. And it's a question that scientists and astronomers have been working to answer ever since space exploration began. They want to know what the Red Planet is really like.

This artist's concept *(above)* shows astronauts using three space shuttles to begin a colony on Mars. This illustration *(right)* depicts the beginning of a Mars colony with living quarters and a greenhouse.

This 2015 image shows the south pole of Mars covered by an ice cap made up of carbon dioxide.

Long before people sent spacecraft to explore Mars, they wondered about the Red Planet. In 1609 the scientist Galileo Galilei was the first person to look at Mars through a telescope. Other astronomers looked at Mars and discovered "white spots" at the poles. In 1719 an Italian astronomer named Giancomo Miraldi wondered if these spots could be ice caps. It would be almost three hundred years before scientists could confirm whether Miraldi's theory was correct.

Early astronomers drew maps of what they saw through their telescopes. In 1877 an Italian astronomer saw dark grooves on Mars's surface. He called them *canali*, meaning "channels." But the word was mistranslated as "canals," so some people began to think that intelligent beings had dug canals on Mars. The fascination with Mars grew. People wrote books, radio plays, and films about Mars and the idea that there could be life there.

Between 1960 and 2016, space agencies attempted to launch forty-four unmanned spacecraft to Mars. Only twenty of these flights were successful. Some failed to launch. Others did not escape Earth's orbit. Problems occurred when solar panels did not open or radios stopped sending signals. Some spacecraft failed to enter Mars's orbit.

Mariner 4 reached Mars in 1965.

Mariner 4 was the first spacecraft to take pictures of another planet.

Others crashed when trying to land. But space organizations continued to plan missions to explore and discover more about this fascinating planet.

▶ FLYBYS AND PHOTOS

The first spacecraft sent to Mars were designed to fly by the planet. They would get close enough to take pictures and radio the images back to Earth. After passing by Mars, their missions would end, and they would orbit the sun. In 1965 NASA's *Mariner 4* was the first craft to successfully fly by Mars. It passed within 6,118 miles (9,846 kilometers) of Mars. That was close enough for *Mariner 4* to take twenty-two photographs to send back to Earth.

These photographs, as well as those from two more successful flybys by *Mariner 6* and *Mariner 7*, showed a planet covered with craters. These flybys also flew over where people had once thought they'd seen channels. But these early photographs showed no canals covering the dry, dusty planet. The scientists who studied the photos thought that Mars probably looked a lot like the moon.

▶ MAPPING IN ORBIT

Mariner 9, launched in 1971, was the next successful mission. It was not a flyby. Instead, the spacecraft had an onboard rocket that thrust it into orbit around Mars. For over a year, *Mariner 9* sent back images and data that it collected as it circled Mars.

Mariner 9 (inset) took pictures of Mars from orbit. A *Mariner 9* photo shows a volcanic region on Mars *(bottom)*.

An artist's concept shows a Martian dust storm.

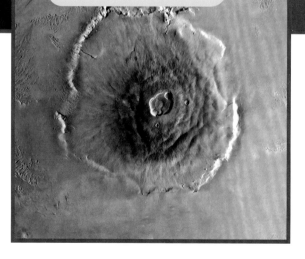

This image *(inset)*, taken by equipment on *Viking 1*, shows a volcano on Mars.

It mapped around 85 percent of the planet's surface and studied the Martian atmosphere.

Mariner 9 changed our view of Mars. The spacecraft reached the planet during a massive dust storm. Only the highest volcanoes and mountains were visible. But when the dust settled, the mapping began. Over the next year, the orbiter took 7,329 images of Mars and its two moons. The photographs showed that there was more to Mars than craters. Mars had volcanoes, mountains, and polar caps. Mars also had massive canyons near its equator. The canyons were more than 2,500 miles (4,020 km) long and up to 6 miles (10 km) deep. Similar landforms on Earth, such as the Grand Canyon, are created by the movement of water. Scientists wondered if these canyons also could have been carved by water. But to find out, they needed more evidence that water once flowed on Mars.

LANDING ON MARS

In the 1970s to 1980s, space agencies made many attempts to land spacecraft on Mars. *Viking 1* and *2* were the first successful missions. These NASA spacecraft had orbiters that entered Mars's orbit. For a month, these orbiters took images, looking for landing sites. Then the landers separated from the orbiters and touched down. The missions were expected to last for ninety days after

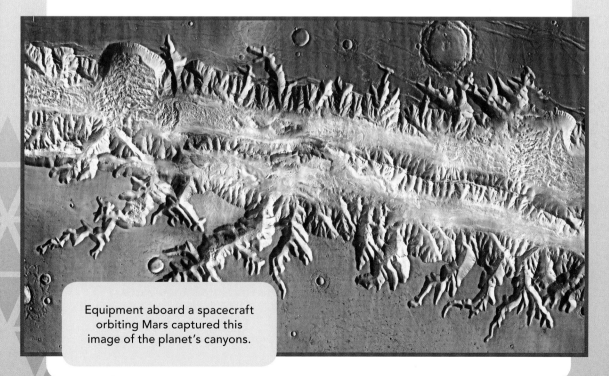

Equipment aboard a spacecraft orbiting Mars captured this image of the planet's canyons.

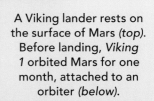

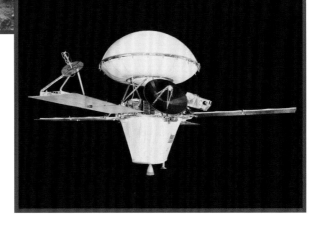

A Viking lander rests on the surface of Mars *(top)*. Before landing, *Viking 1* orbited Mars for one month, attached to an orbiter *(below)*.

landing. But the orbiters and landers continued to send data to Earth for several years.

Along with photographing Mars, the landers looked for evidence of life. They scooped up and analyzed Martian soil. Scientists were surprised to find chemicals similar to those found in Earth's soil. But the landers did not find any evidence of living organisms.

Although the landers could not prove that there was life on Mars, they discovered many new things. They detected water vapor in the atmosphere and frozen water in the polar ice caps. They observed weather patterns. They found that temperatures could be as low as −184°F (−120°C). These observations were important not only for understanding Mars but also for planning future missions. Astronomers learned that if humans were ever to travel to Mars, they would have to watch out for dust storms. And they would have to be prepared for extreme temperatures and dangerous radiation.

▶ ROVING THE RED PLANET

The next step in exploring Mars was to send a lander with a vehicle. The lander would have instruments to conduct experiments. The vehicle, called a rover, would be able to move across the surface of the planet. In 1997 a lander known as

This artist's concept depicts the first Mars rover after landing.

Pathfinder reached Mars. It carried a rover named *Sojourner*. Parachutes slowed *Pathfinder*'s descent. Huge air bags let it land safely. It bounced like a beach ball before coming to rest. After the landing, *Sojourner* rolled down a ramp. It drove away from *Pathfinder* and began exploring.

The mission's goal was to demonstrate the technology needed to send a lander and a rover to Mars. *Pathfinder* and *Sojourner* easily completed this goal. It was the first time a spacecraft had landed using these parachutes and air bags. The lander and rover also lasted much longer than scientists planned for and sent back much more data than scientists expected. For two and a half months, *Sojourner* collected data about soil and rocks as it traveled about 330 feet (100 meters). *Pathfinder* took images of whirlwinds called dust devils. It found ice clouds in the mornings.

Pathfinder and *Sojourner* successfully reached Mars in 1997.

By afternoon the ice had evaporated. Scientists studied *Pathfinder*'s data. They learned that Mars was dry and cold. But the data suggested that Mars might once have been warm and wet.

While *Pathfinder* and *Sojourner* explored Mars, another orbiter arrived. For the next ten years, the *Mars Global Surveyor* orbited and mapped the entire planet. The *Surveyor*'s data helped scientists decide where to send the next rovers. These rovers would search for water on Mars.

Evaporating ice on Mars created this spidery terrain of channels.

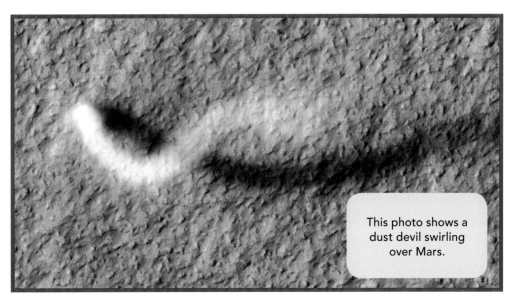

This photo shows a dust devil swirling over Mars.

Nearly 71 percent of Earth is covered by water. When viewed from space, most of the planet looks blue.

In pictures of Earth taken from space, the planet looks blue. Oceans, lakes, and rivers cover Earth. Every living thing on Earth needs water. Scientists assume that the same would be true of living things on another planet. One way to find past or present life on Mars is to search for evidence of water.

Unlike Earth, Mars is cold, dusty, and dry. But scientists suspect that billions of years ago, Earth and Mars may have been more similar. Mars might have been warmer and wetter. If water once covered Mars the way it covers Earth, then possibly Mars was also filled with living things.

For many years, the focus of Mars exploration was to Follow the Water. This search made a giant leap forward in 2002 when

Mars may have once been warm and wet. But the planet is cold, dusty, and dry.

the orbiter *Mars Odyssey* discovered water ice below the surface of Mars near its south pole. Scientists were surprised to find enough ice to fill Lake Michigan twice. "This is the best direct evidence we have of subsurface water ice on Mars," said William Boynton of the University of Arizona. "What we have found is much more ice than we ever expected."

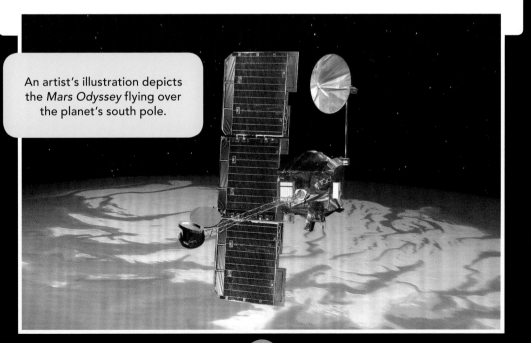

An artist's illustration depicts the *Mars Odyssey* flying over the planet's south pole.

This discovery was just the beginning. *Odyssey* continues to orbit and study Mars, and it works with two rovers sent to Mars to continue the search for water.

SPIRIT AND *OPPORTUNITY*

In January 2004, two spacecraft with rovers landed on opposite sides of Mars. The rovers, *Spirit* and *Opportunity*, were designed to answer questions about the history of water on Mars. Scientists planned for these rovers to work for three months. But *Spirit* roamed the planet until 2010. In 2014 *Opportunity* set the record for the longest distance traveled by an off-world rover. In 2015 it completed the first off-world marathon, having traveled more than 26 miles (42 km) in just over eleven years.

Each rover is about the size of a golf cart, with six wheels and a suspension system that lets it roll over rocks. The rovers are almost 5 feet (1.5 m) tall. They are heavy enough to withstand

Spirit and *Opportunity* were designed to be able to travel easily over Mars's rocky surface. This illustration shows one of the rovers on Mars.

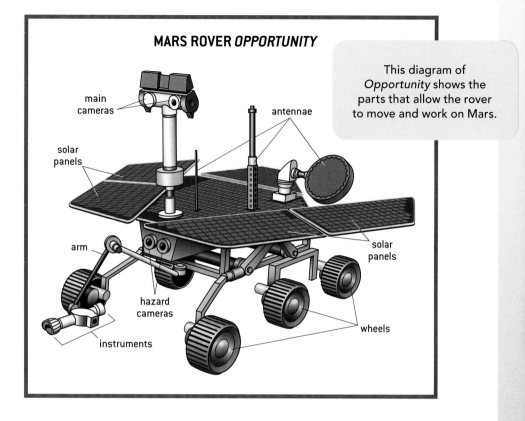

MARS ROVER *OPPORTUNITY*

main cameras

solar panels

antennae

This diagram of *Opportunity* shows the parts that allow the rover to move and work on Mars.

arm

solar panels

hazard cameras

instruments

wheels

strong winds. A rotating panoramic camera sits at the top of a mast on each rover. The cameras send images to a computer inside the rover. The computer then sends the data to the *Odyssey* orbiter in space, which sends it to Earth. Once a day, scientists on Earth send commands back to the orbiter. It transmits them to the rovers. Scientists control the rovers, but they are powered by batteries. Solar panels charge the batteries. With a full charge, the rovers can travel more than 300 feet (100 m) a day.

Spirit and *Opportunity* are robot geologists. They study rocks and soil to find clues about water. Scientists use a rover's camera to spot landforms that might have been formed by water. The rover's robotic arm holds its scientific instruments. A microscopic camera lets scientists look at landforms close up. Another tool works like a hammer. It grinds open rocks to study what is inside. Some of the instruments figure out which minerals make up the rocks and soils on Mars. They also measure air temperature and collect magnetic particles.

Spirit and *Opportunity* landed in places that scientists thought might have evidence of water. The scientists made their decisions based on information collected by the *Mars Global Surveyor* spacecraft. *Opportunity* landed on a flat plain named Meridiani Planum. Within six weeks, *Opportunity* identified layers of rocks and minerals that form in water. Scientists determined that the plain was once the bottom of a shallow sea.

Opportunity later came across BB-sized pellets scattered on the ground. They looked like tiny blueberries. "There are features in this soil unlike anything ever seen on Mars before," said Steve Squyres, the chief scientist for the rover's mission. The rover's instruments showed that the "blueberries" were actually a mineral called hematite. On Earth, hematite forms in places with

Opportunity landed on Meridiani Planum, shown here. The plain may have once been the bottom of a sea.

water. Scientists thought the hematite on Mars may have come from groundwater.

 Spirit soon found signs of water too. It landed in an area that scientists thought might once have been a lake. Instead, the area turned out to be a lava field with no signs of water. So Spirit climbed to some small hills almost 2 miles (3 km) away. When one of its wheels stopped turning, the rover began to drive in reverse.

Opportunity captured this image of hematite on Mars.

This image, from the camera on top of *Spirit*, shows the trench dug by the rover's broken wheel.

As it moved, the broken wheel dug a trench. Inside the trench, *Spirit* discovered that the soil was made mostly of silica. On Earth, silica forms when hot water reacts with rocks. As *Spirit* continued exploring, it found more silica. Scientists think that steam might have once bubbled up through silica-covered cracks in the rocks. Vents like these on Earth are full of tiny life-forms called microbes. It is possible that similar microbes also lived in these vents on Mars.

Eventually, *Spirit* fell into a sand dune. Scientists sent commands to *Spirit* to try to free the rover, but they were unsuccessful. As it tried to move, *Spirit*'s spinning wheels broke through the Martian crust. With no way to travel, *Spirit* started looking closely at the layers of sand where it rested. Each layer showed materials that form in water. Scientists think that snow once fell in the place where *Spirit* sits. The warm soil under the snow would have made the bottom layers of snow melt, allowing it to seep into the ground.

During the next Martian winter, *Spirit*'s solar panels were tilted away from the sun. It could not recharge its batteries, and it stopped sending signals to Earth. But *Opportunity* continued to explore Mars.

▶ AN ANCIENT STREAM

Two years after *Spirit* stopped communicating with Earth, yet another rover was sent to Mars. *Curiosity*'s goal was to find evidence of life, but within one month of landing, the rover had made its own exciting discovery about water on Mars.

Scientists sent *Curiosity* to explore two rocky areas, known as Hottah and Link. When *Curiosity* sent photos back to Earth, scientists noticed smaller stones and gravel trapped within the larger rocks. They determined that the rock was part of an ancient streambed. The stones and gravel were as smooth and round as gravel found in rivers on Earth. "The shapes tell you they were transported and the sizes tell you they couldn't be transported by wind. They were transported by water flow," said Rebecca Williams of the Planetary Science Institute in Arizona. For the first time, scientists had evidence of flowing water on Mars. Later, scientists compared images and data from some dark streaks seen on the surface of Mars. And in 2015, they announced that water still flows on the Red Planet.

CHAPTER 3
THE SEARCH FOR LIFE

A camera on a Mars orbiter captured this image revealing mineral deposits in a Martian valley.

After so many signs of water were discovered on Mars, NASA moved on to another exploration strategy, called Seek Signs of Life. The *Curiosity* rover that landed in 2012 is one of the first steps in the new project. Scientists chose to land *Curiosity* in an area where signs of water had been seen. Then *Curiosity* could start its mission of studying its surroundings for signs that life once inhabited the area. The rover studies rocks and soil to learn about the past geology and climate of Mars. It looks for the ingredients such as carbon or other chemicals that are necessary to support life.

A series of images taken by *Curiosity* were stitched together to create this self-portrait of the rover.

SATISFYING OUR *CURIOSITY*

Curiosity is about the size of a small SUV. It is twice as long and five times as heavy as previous rovers. Designed to be an explorer, *Curiosity* has all the tools it needs to work on Mars. Two computers act as the rover's brains. Six wheels and a suspension system let it drive over rocky terrain. The rover's tall mast holds two pairs of "eyes"—navigation cameras that take images to send to scientists on Earth. Other cameras examine rocks and avoid hazards. The rover's arm and hand scoop soil and prepare samples. The arm delivers samples to

A camera on the *Curiosity* rover captured this image of its first scoop of Martian sand.

This artist's concept shows *Curiosity* examining a rock using the instruments on its arm.

glassy sphere

glassy ellipsoid

reddish gray

gray

glassy sphere

nearly white

clear, translucent

A close-up photo taken by *Curiosity* shows different kinds of sand observed on Mars.

instruments inside the rover's body. The instruments analyze the chemistry of rocks, soil, and the atmosphere. Three antennae serve as *Curiosity*'s voice and ears. The rover communicates with NASA's orbiters, and they relay messages to Earth. Instead of solar panels, *Curiosity* uses plutonium for fuel. Because it does not depend on the sun, it does not lose power during dust storms or run low on energy in the winter.

Curiosity had success with the first sample it drilled in 2013. The rover had traveled about 1,600 feet (490 m) from where it landed. There it drilled into rocks that had once been the bottom of a lake. The rover analyzed the powdery sample. It found that the rock had been deposited in freshwater, where living things can thrive. Before this, all the evidence pointed to Mars having salty and acidic water that might have been too harsh for microbes to live. *Curiosity*'s instruments also found carbon, sulfur, and oxygen. These are some of the chemical ingredients that living things require. "A fundamental question for this mission is whether Mars could have supported a habitable environment," said Michael Meyer, lead scientist for NASA's Mars Exploration Program. "From what we know now, the answer is yes."

A self-portrait of *Curiosity* shows the rover at a Martian sand dune.

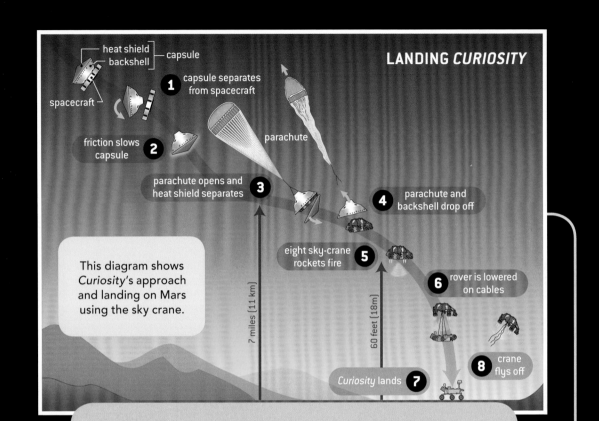

LANDING CURIOSITY

heat shield
backshell — capsule

spacecraft

1 capsule separates from spacecraft

2 friction slows capsule

3 parachute opens and heat shield separates

parachute

4 parachute and backshell drop off

5 eight sky-crane rockets fire

6 rover is lowered on cables

This diagram shows *Curiosity*'s approach and landing on Mars using the sky crane.

7 miles (11 km)

60 feet (18m)

7 *Curiosity* lands

8 crane flys off

Landing *Curiosity*

To land *Curiosity* on Mars, NASA had to come up with a new technique. Other rovers landed using giant air bags to cushion their fall. One lander used rockets to slowly land on three legs. But *Curiosity* was too big and heavy to use these techniques. *Curiosity* would need to land gently and without kicking up too much dust to avoid destroying the rover and its tools. So engineers designed a complex landing system with a sky crane and rockets. They couldn't test the system before they used it, so nobody was quite sure if the seemingly crazy method would work. NASA scientists began calling *Curiosity*'s landing "seven minutes of terror."

After about eight months of cruising through space to reach Mars, it was time to land *Curiosity*. As its spacecraft approached the Martian atmosphere, a capsule holding the rover and sky crane separated from the craft. The capsule was made up of a heat shield and backshell. The outside temperature was 3,800°F (2,093°C). But the shield kept the rover safe and cool. Friction from the atmosphere slowed the capsule from 13,200 to 1,000 miles (21,243 to 1,609 km) per hour. At 7 miles (11 km) aboveground, a huge parachute opened, and the heat shield detached. The capsule slowed to 200 miles (322 km) per hour. Then the parachute and backshell dropped off. Eight rockets on the sky crane fired, allowing *Curiosity* to hover 60 feet (18 m) above the surface. Then *Curiosity* dropped down, dangling from strong cables attached to the sky crane. The rover's six wheels and suspension system popped into place, and *Curiosity*'s wheels touched down. When the rover detected that it had landed, it cut the cables from the sky crane, and the crane flew away and crash-landed in another area.

An artist's rendering shows the sky crane lowering *Curiosity* onto the surface of Mars.

Curiosity's success continued. Upon drilling another rock, it found organic molecules. Organic molecules, which contain carbon and hydrogen, are often called the building blocks of life. But these molecules can also exist in nonliving things. They might have formed on Mars. Or a meteorite could have brought the molecules to Mars. The compounds do not prove that there has been life on Mars. But they are further evidence of an environment that living things could inhabit.

After completing its initial mission, *Curiosity* began to climb a nearby mountain in 2014. There it compares different layers of rocks on the mountain. Researchers are looking at how the Martian environment has changed over time. The ancient layers of rocks were formed in a wet habitat where microbes could have survived. They differ sharply from the harsher, drier conditions that ruled Mars when younger rocks formed.

Curiosity captured this image showing various layers of rock in Mount Sharp. The layers below the white dots appear to have formed in a wet environment.

This map shows *Curiosity*'s route in April and May 2015. The numbers represent Martian days as counted since the rover landed on Mars.

An image taken by *Curiosity* shows veins that may have formed by fluids flowing through the rocks.

Curiosity's research has shown that Mars once had an environment where living things could survive. It continues to study the planet's geology and climate. The next Martian rover, planned for 2020, will continue the search for life on Mars.

CHAPTER 4
JOURNEY TO MARS

Astronauts on the ISS are conducting research to prepare for missions in deep space. This inflatable module may be used for storage or housing in future space travel.

In 2015 NASA released a report outlining its plan to send a manned mission to Mars by the 2030s. NASA said that because Mars and Earth are similar in their composition and changing seasons, further exploration of Mars will help scientists understand even more about Earth's history and future. This research will also help scientists answer questions about life beyond Earth. The NASA report noted that scientists on the ISS and on Earth are completing research to further understand space and develop the technology necessary for humans to reach Mars. NASA also has plans to visit an asteroid in 2025 so that astronomers can learn more about traveling through deep space.

NASA plans to send manned missions into deep space in preparation for a mission to Mars.

Many people, including some scientists and government officials, are skeptical of this plan. They say that it would make more sense for humans to visit the moon again. They doubt that humans will be able to reach Mars.

Despite the naysayers, NASA isn't giving up on its goal. NASA administrator Charles Bolden gave a speech at the National Space Symposium in 2016 urging people to understand why Mars matters. Bolden said that before people went to the moon, many thought it was a crazy and impossible idea. But astronauts did achieve that goal. Bolden thinks the same could happen for Mars.

Charles Bolden speaks at the National Space Symposium in 2016.

LEARNING ABOARD THE SPACE STATION

To prepare for future missions to Mars, astronauts on the ISS are experimenting with new kinds of spacecraft, living quarters, and even food supplies. They'll need these technologies to travel beyond Earth's orbit.

One of the most important things to know about before sending astronauts to Mars is how long journeys through space might affect the human body. One astronaut, Scott Kelly, spent nearly an entire year aboard the ISS. His twin brother, Mark, stayed on Earth. Throughout the year, both twins gave samples of blood, urine, and saliva so scientists could test how Scott's body reacted to a year in orbit. Scientists' findings will help astronauts know how to prepare for future long-term missions through space.

Scientists also know that there is radiation in space and on Mars, so they are working to figure out what radiation does to the body and how to avoid contact with dangerous levels

Scott Kelly floats aboard the ISS, where he lived for almost one year.

Kelly cares for plants on the ISS *(top)*. Astronaut Tim Peake is excited to have fresh fruit during his time on the ISS *(inset)*.

of radiation. Other scientists are working on creating a space suit that will be flexible enough to allow astronauts to move and bend easily and that will protect them from radiation and extreme temperatures.

Another concern about long trips in space is how to make sure that astronauts have enough water and food. Some scientists on the ISS have been growing vegetables with the help of LED lights and injections of water. They are also studying Martian soil to figure out how to grow food on Mars. Being able to grow fresh food in space would make long journeys more enjoyable

Astronauts aboard the ISS grew this lettuce.

and easier for the body to handle. Not only would it provide something for astronauts to do, but plants also produce oxygen that people need to breathe.

Scientists on the ISS also find ways to use and access water. Scientists have figured out that the Martian atmosphere is much more humid than they once thought, so it may become easier to get water on Mars. But scientists can purify sweat and urine to make drinkable water for astronauts. And water can be split into oxygen and hydrogen molecules. This may help keep enough breathable oxygen in the air.

Before a human crew flies to Mars, they will send several supply rockets. A lightweight, inflatable module might be used to carry cargo. This type of module was first sent to the ISS in 2016. When it is filled with air and expanded, astronauts will test radiation levels, temperature, and how well it withstands impact for two years. The inflatable modules might someday be used to house people in deep space.

In *The Martian*, Matt Damon plays an astronaut stranded on Mars.

Farming on Mars

In the 2015 movie *The Martian*, an astronaut stranded on Mars figures out how to grow potatoes to help him survive. Scientists on Earth are trying to figure out if food can be grown in Martian soil. But these scientists don't have access to real Martian soil. So instead, they created some.

Using data collected by Mars missions, scientists were able to mimic the conditions of Martian soil. After mixing in some organic materials from Earth, they were able to successfully grow peas and tomatoes. The scientists haven't proven yet whether their soil behaves the way soil on Mars does or if the vegetables are safe for humans to eat. But many scientists agree that one day potatoes could really grow on Mars.

DEEP-SPACE EXPLORATION

Before journeying to Mars, astronauts will take other trips to deep space. The *Orion* spacecraft is being designed to carry astronauts. A powerful Space Launch System (SLS) rocket will launch *Orion*. The launcher will stand taller than the Statue of Liberty. It will have as much power as 160,000 Corvette engines. The first SLS mission will be flown without a crew. *Orion* will orbit the moon and return to Earth after about twenty-five days. The second mission will take a crew of four on a similar journey.

NASA plans to fly astronauts in *Orion* to an asteroid in the 2020s. That journey will help scientists to understand the technology needed to send people into deep space for longer periods of time. Eventually missions will orbit Mars or land on one of the Martian moons. Someday *Orion* will take astronauts to the surface of Mars.

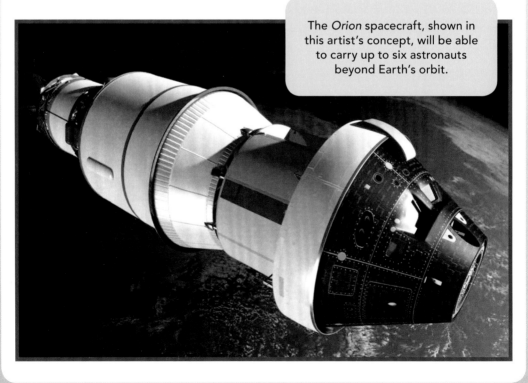

The *Orion* spacecraft, shown in this artist's concept, will be able to carry up to six astronauts beyond Earth's orbit.

BRINGING MARS TO EARTH

It will be many years before scientists solve the technical problems of traveling to Mars. Maybe someday you will be able to journey to Mars. But before then, you might be able to see yourself on the Red Planet.

NASA has created a "mixed reality" tour of Mars. The tour mixes real and virtual worlds. Wearing a headset, visitors to the NASA Kennedy Space Center in Florida can see Mars as if they were really there. The virtual Martian world is constructed from images taken by *Curiosity*. A holograph of Buzz Aldrin, the second astronaut to walk on the moon, guides part of the tour of Mars.

Tourists are not the only ones who view Martian mixed reality. *Curiosity* scientists use the tool. It helps them decide where to send the rover and choose rock formations to study. For some *Curiosity* scientists, the mixed reality headsets give them the sense that they are really working on Mars.

A holograph of a driver for *Curiosity* leads visitors across a virtual Mars.

WHAT'S NEXT?

A new rover is set to launch in 2020. It will launch when Earth's orbit and Mars's orbit bring the two planets closer together. *Mars 2020* will have many of the design features of *Curiosity*. It will land in a site that might have been habitable in the past. The rover will continue the mission of studying whether life could exist on Mars. It will also search for direct evidence of past life.

In addition to investigating Mars, the new rover will collect and store samples of rocks and soils. No spacecraft has yet returned to Earth from Mars. But someday the samples collected by *Mars 2020* might be brought back to Earth.

The *Mars 2020* rover, shown in this sketch, will be similar to *Curiosity* but have updated scientific instruments to search for evidence of life.

#JOURNEYTOMARS

Missions such as the one planned for 2020 will help scientists prepare for the biggest mission yet: sending humans to Mars.

The 2020 rover will also prepare for future human exploration on Mars. One of the instruments on the rover will collect carbon dioxide from the Martian atmosphere. It will compress and store the gas. Then it will split the gas to release oxygen. The oxygen might someday be used for rocket fuel or for people to breathe. If this experiment is successful, humans will be one step closer to being able to travel to Mars.

Source Notes

6 Mike Wall, "Now Is the Time to Colonize Mars, Elon Musk Says," *Space.com*, December 16, 2015, http://www.space.com/31388-elon-musk-colonize-mars-now.html.

6 Ross Anderson, "Exodus," *Aeon*, September 30, 2014, https://aeon.co/essays/elon-musk-puts-his-case-for-a-multi-planet-civilisation.

18–19 "Found It! Ice on Mars," NASA, May 28, 2002, http://science.nasa.gov/science-news/science-at-nasa/2002/28may_marsice.

22 NASA, "*Opportunity* Sees Tiny Spheres in Martian Soil," news release, February 4, 2004, http://mars.nasa.gov/mer/newsroom/pressreleases/20040204a.html.

25 NASA, "NASA Rover Finds Old Streambed on Martian Surface," news release, September 27, 2012, http://mars.nasa.gov/msl/news/whatsnew/index.cfm?FuseAction=ShowNews&NewsID=1360.

29 "NASA Rover Finds Conditions Once Suited for Ancient Life on Mars," NASA, March 12, 2013, http://mars.nasa.gov/msl/news/whatsnew/index.cfm?FuseAction=ShowNews&NewsID=1438.

30 Daniel Honan, "Seven Minutes of Terror: Engineering the Mars Rover's Impossible Landing," *Big Think*, accessed May 11, 2016, http://bigthink.com/think-tank/mars-rover-landings-seven-minutes-of-terror.

Glossary

atmosphere: the layer of gases surrounding a planet

canyon: a deep valley with steep sides. Canyons are often carved by water.

carbon: a chemical element found in all living plants and animals

crater: a large, round hole formed by the impact of a meteor

data: facts or pieces of information

evidence: items that prove or disprove something

habitable: able to be lived in

meteorite: a mass of stone that reaches Earth or another planet from outer space

microbe: an organism that is too small to be seen without a microscope

mineral: a substance that is naturally formed underground

orbit: the path taken by a planet around the sun or a spacecraft around a planet. When a spacecraft circles a planet or the moon, this is called orbiting.

organic: related to or coming from living things

radiation: particles that are emitted in nuclear decay. High levels of radiation can be harmful to humans.

robotic: a machine that operates automatically with humanlike skill

silica: a compound that occurs in sand and quartz

suspension: a system of tires, springs, and shock absorbers that connects a vehicle to its wheels and allows motion between the two

unmanned: not controlled by a crew

Selected Bibliography

"All about Mars: History." NASA. Accessed May 11, 2016. http://mars.nasa.gov /allaboutmars/mystique/history.

"Mars Science Laboratory/*Curiosity*." NASA. Accessed May 11, 2016. http:// mars.nasa.gov/msl/news/pdfs/MSL_Fact_Sheet.pdf.

NASA. "NASA Confirms Evidence That Liquid Water Flows on Today's Mars." News release, September 28, 2015. http://www.nasa.gov/press-release /nasa-confirms-evidence-that-liquid-water-flows-on-today-s-mars.

———. "NASA Releases Plan Outlining Next Steps in the Journey to Mars." News release, October 8, 2015. https://www.nasa.gov/press-release /nasa-releases-plan-outlining-next-steps-in-the-journey-to-mars.

"*Spirit and Opportunity*." Exploratorium. Accessed May 11, 2016. http://www .exploratorium.edu/mars/spiritopp.php.

Further Reading

Aldrin, Buzz, and Marianne J. Dyson. *Welcome to Mars: Making a Home on the Red Planet*. Washington, DC: National Geographic, 2015.

"Animation of Site of Seasonal Flows of Water in Hale Crater, Mars" https://www.youtube.com/watch?v=MDb3UZPoTpc

Cornell, Kari. *Mars Science Lab Engineer Diana Trujillo*. Minneapolis: Lerner Publications, 2016.

Curiosity Rover https://www.nasa.gov/mission_pages/msl/index.html

Lee, Pascal. *Mission: Mars*. New York: Scholastic, 2013.

Miller, Ron. *Curiosity's Mission on Mars*. Minneapolis: Twenty-First Century Books, 2014.

NASA: Journey to Mars http://www.nasa.gov/topics/journeytomars/index.html

Index

Photo Acknowledgments

The images in this book are used with the permission of: NASA, pp. 2, 10, 14 (right), 16, 19 (top), 20, 33 (top), 37 (top), 38, 40, 41; © MR1805/iStock/ Thinkstock, p. 4; © Bruce Weaver/AFP/Getty Images, p. 5 (top); © Patrick T. Fallon/Bloomberg/Getty Images, p. 5 (bottom); AP Photo/Rex Features, p. 6; NASA/Case for Mars, p. 7 (all); ESA, p. 8; © NASA/National Geographic/ Getty Images, p. 9 (top); AP Photo/NASA, p. 9 (bottom); © Time Life Pictures/ NASA/The LIFE Picture Collection/Getty Images, p. 11 (top); © NASA/Getty Images, p. 11 (bottom); © Detlev van Ravenswaay/Science Source, p. 12 (top); NASA/Jody Swann/Tammy Becker/Alfred McEwen, p. 12; NASA/JPL-Caltech / University of Arizona, pp. 13, 17 (top), 26; © SPL/Science Source, p. 14 (left); © Time Life Pictures/NASA/Getty Images, p. 15; © Science Source, p. 17 (bottom); © sdecoret/Shutterstock.com, p. 18; © Science Source, p. 19 (bottom); © Laura Westlund/Independent Picture Service, p. 21; NASA/ JPL-Caltech/Cornell Univ./Arizona State Univ., pp. 22 (bottom), 23 (bottom); © NASA/Science Source, p. 23 (top); NASA/JPL-Caltech, pp. 24, 28 (all), 42; NASA/JPL-Caltech/MSSS, p. 27 (all), 29, 32, 33 (bottom), 43; © Laura Westlund/ Independent Picture Service via NASA, p. 30; NASA/JPL, p. 31; NASA/ Bigelow Aerospace, p. 32; NASA/Jim Grossman, p. 35 (top); © Matthew Staver/ Bloomberg/Getty Images, p. 35 (bottom); ESA/NASA, pp. 36, 37 (bottom); © Atlaspix/Alamy, p. 39.

Front cover: NASA.